Short Reading Passages & Graphic Organizers to Build Comprehension

GRADES 4-5

By Linda Ward Beech

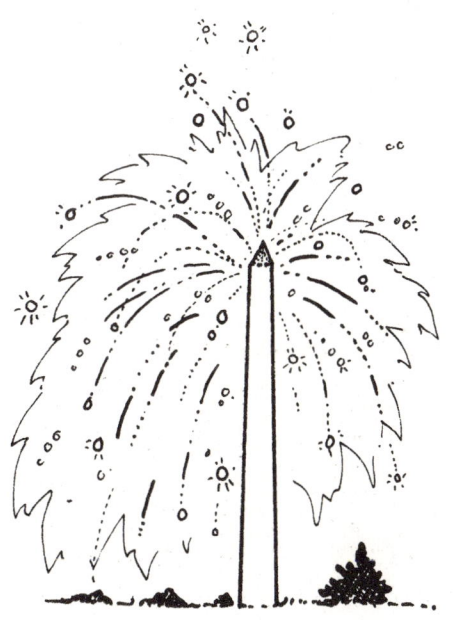

SCHOLASTIC
PROFESSIONAL BOOKS

New York • Toronto • London • Auckland • Sydney
Mexico City • New Delhi • Hong Kong • Buenos Aires

Teachers may photocopy the designated reproducible pages for classroom use. No other part of this publication
may be reproduced in whole or in part, or stored in a retrieval system, or transmitted in any form or by any means
electronic, mechanical, photocopying, recording or otherwise, without written permission of the publisher.
For information regarding permission, write to Scholastic Inc., 555 Broadway, New York, NY 10012.

Cover design by Kelli Thompson (based on a design by Daniel Moreton)
Interior design by Sydney Wright
Interior illustration by Maxie Chambliss

ISBN: 0-439-16357-9

Copyright © 2001 by Linda Ward Beech. All rights reserved.

Printed in the U.S.A.

Contents

To the Teacher 4

Concept Webs/Topic and Main Idea
Remember This 6
Fine Fingerprints 7
Dutch Treats 8
Slippery Slopes in the Seas 9
July 4th Events 10
Get the Point 11
Bird Words 12
On the Radar Screen 13
Food for Thought 14
Testing It Out 15

Hierarchical Webs/Classifying
Musical Notes 16
Let's Rock 17
House Words 18
Short For .19
Counting Calories 20
Preview of Prefixes 21
Eating in Egypt 22
Testing It Out 23

Time Lines/Sequence
Best Books 24
Colorful Events 25

Trees of History 26
Many Milestones 27
Time for Sports 28
Jersey Firsts 29
Presidential Passages 30
Testing It Out 31

Venn Diagrams/Comparing
Double Dakota 32
Into the Woods 33
Catch This 34
Temperature Tales 35
Venus Visit 36
Out in Front 37
Many Thanks 38
Testing It Out 39

Cause-and-Effect Maps/Relationships
The Elves of Iceland 40
Address Unknown 41
Moonwalkers on City Streets 42
The Real McCoy 43
A Cold Fish 44
Plans, Please 45
It's Corny .46
Testing It Out 47

Answers .48

To the Teacher

About the Graphic Organizers

Many students are visual learners and can benefit greatly from using graphic organizers with their reading. Graphic organizers are especially helpful in identifying and sorting information.

As students complete a graphic organizer, they do the following:
- create a visual product based on their reading
- engage in understanding information from a passage
- see relationships among words, facts, and ideas
- gain a sense of purpose and control over their reading
- learn to paraphrase what they read

This book provides high-interest passages for students to read and then break down on a variety of graphic organizers. The following kinds of graphic organizers are included:
- **concept webs** that focus on main ideas and supporting details
- **hierarchical webs** that focus on classifying information
- **time lines** that focus on chronological events
- **Venn diagrams** that focus on making comparisons
- **cause-and-effect maps** that focus on identifying relationships between events

Using the Book

TEACHER TIP

Remind students to use the passage title as a clue to the topic or main idea of a paragraph.

This book is organized so that the first pages of each kind of graphic aid are easier and offer more support. For instance, the concept web on page 6 includes the topic and one detail. The concept web on page 13, however, requires students to decide what the paragraph topic is and to identify six examples that tell about the topic.

As students become familiar with a graphic organizer, encourage them to use their own words and phrases. Point out that there is often more than one way to group information from a passage. For example, on page 11, students might present information in different ways as shown on the next page.

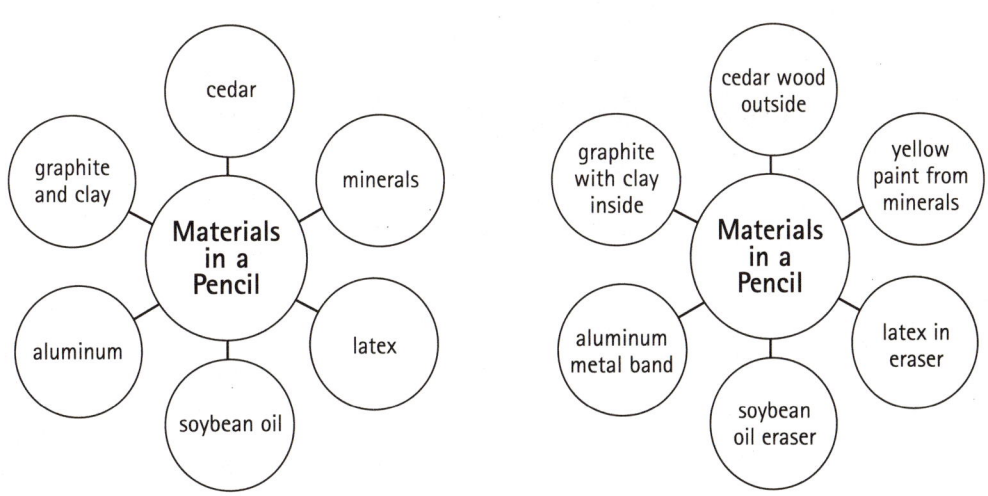

Each graphic organizer page concludes with an activity. Use these MORE! activities to extend and expand students' learning.

By building graphic organizers, students are more likely to understand and retain information for reports, quizzes, tests, and discussions. Each section of the book concludes with a page called **Testing It Out**. The test questions are always based on the passage on the preceding page. Students can easily see the relationship between creating a graphic organizer and using that information on a test.

Other Suggestions

* Because of the limited amount of space on each page, you may want to make enlarged copies of some graphic organizers for students to use. You may also suggest that they draw larger versions of the graphic organizers on separate sheets of paper.

* If students are unfamiliar with a graphic organizer, model its use before assigning the page. Think aloud as you read the passage, directions, and questions, and as you fill in the organizer.

* Encourage students to explain their thinking as they complete the organizers.

* Have students work in cooperative groups to complete some pages. Assign roles such as reader (one who reads the passage to the group), highlighter (one who highlights relevant parts of the passage), mapper (one who fills in the graphic organizer), and checker (one who reviews the completed graphic organizer to be sure it is correct). Encourage group members to switch roles.

Name _____ Date _____

Remember This

At the Olympic Games, people compete in sports. At the World Memory Championships known as the Memoriad, people use their memories to compete. For instance, they study and then try to recall 100 names and faces. In another event, contestants memorize strings of numbers. Other events include memorizing a 50-line poem and recalling the order of a deck of cards. You might say that the Memoriad is an unforgettable competition!

Look at the topic in the web. Find details from the paragraph that tell about the topic. Write them in the web. One detail is given.

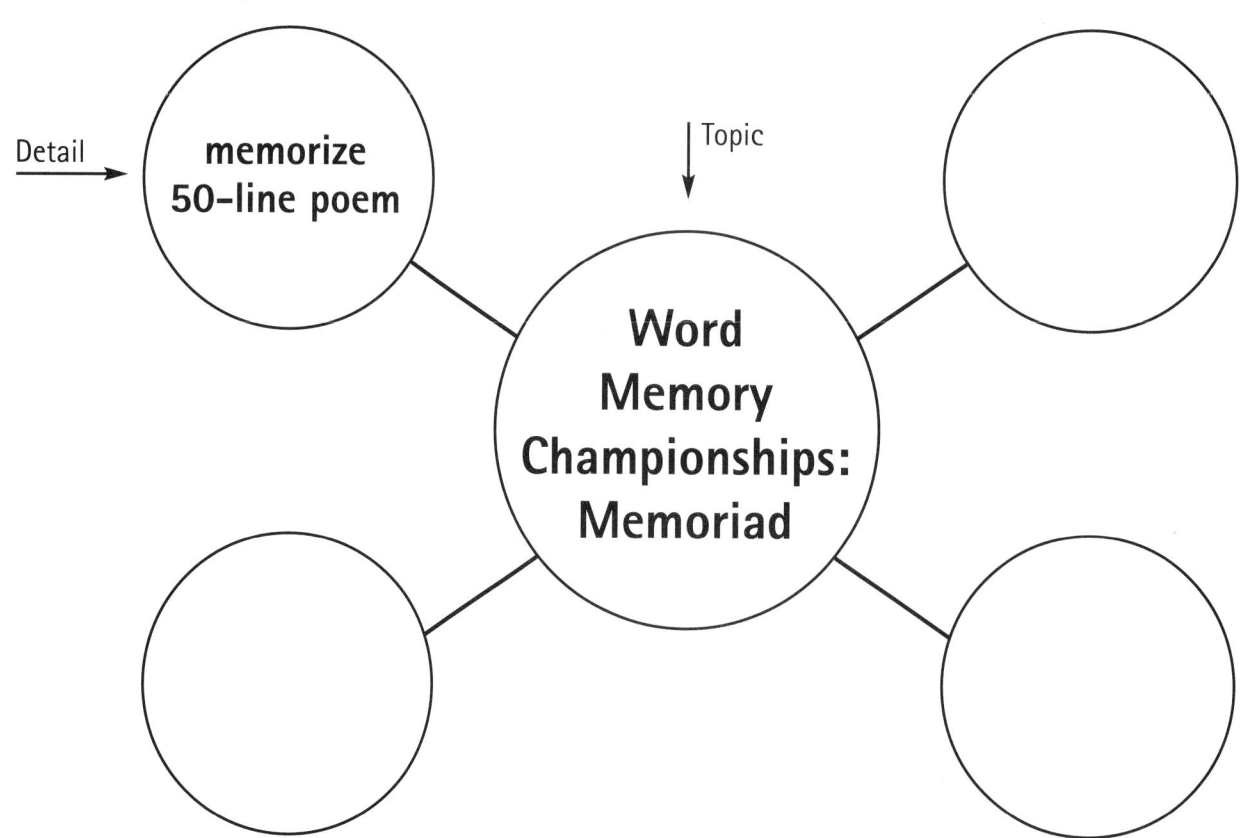

MORE! Find a poem that you like. Memorize it. How long does it take to memorize?

Name _____ Date _____

Fine Fingerprints

Do you know how your fingerprints are like your signature? Both tell who you are. Although each person's fingerprints are unique, fingerprints fall into four main types. Whorl fingerprints look like circles within circles. The ridges on Arch fingerprints look like gentle hills. Tented Arch prints look like very steep hills. The fourth type of fingerprint is known as the Loop. The lines in this type of fingerprint curve around and form patterns that resemble loops.

Arch   Loop

Tented Arch   Whorl

Look at the topic in the web. Find details from the paragraph that tell about the topic. Write them in the web. One detail is given.

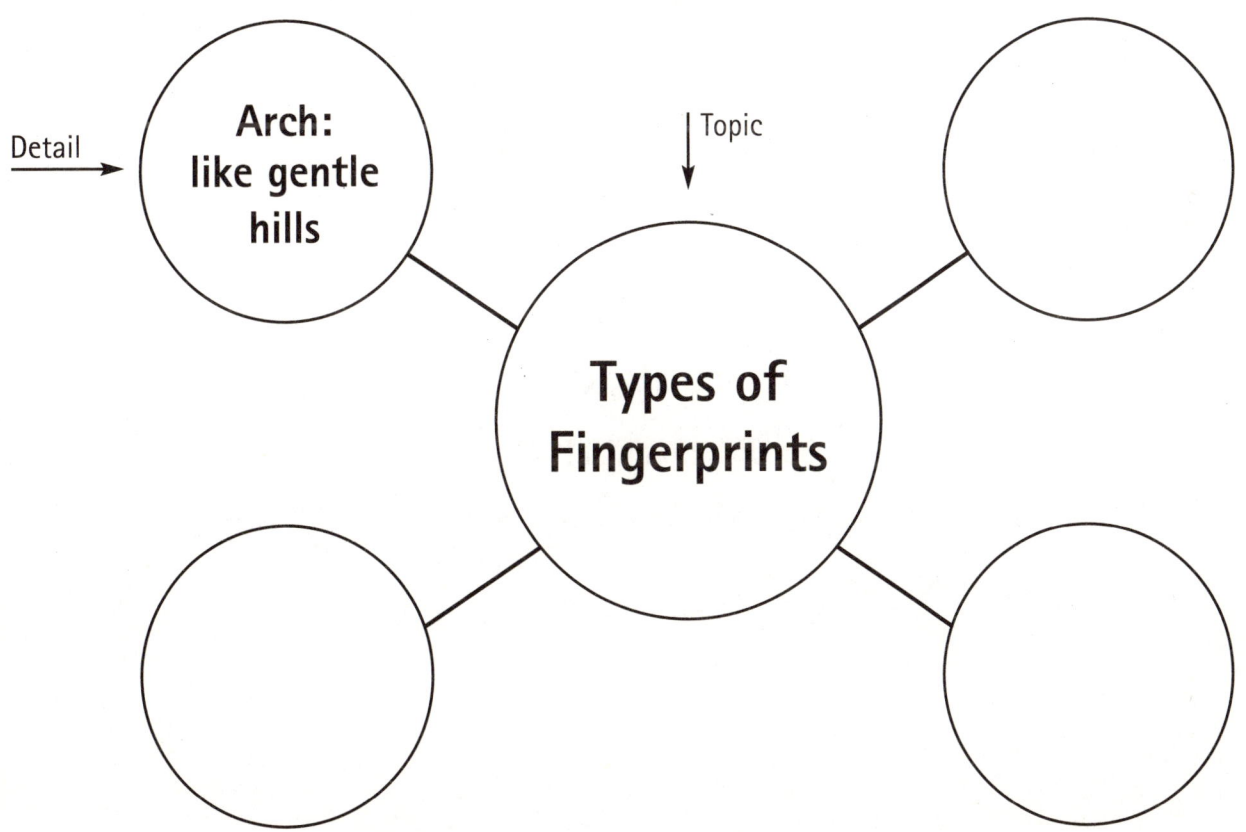

MORE! Find out what types of fingerprints you and your classmates have.

7

Name _____ Date _____

Dutch Treats

The Dutch first came to North America in the 1600s. They brought many Dutch customs to their new home, including some lively ways to have fun. The Dutch introduced the pastimes of ice skating and sleigh riding. Another Dutch amusement that quickly caught on was the game of ninepins. Today, this game is known as bowling. The Dutch also introduced the custom of dying Easter eggs.

Look at the topic in the web. Find details from the paragraph that tell about the topic. Write them in the web.

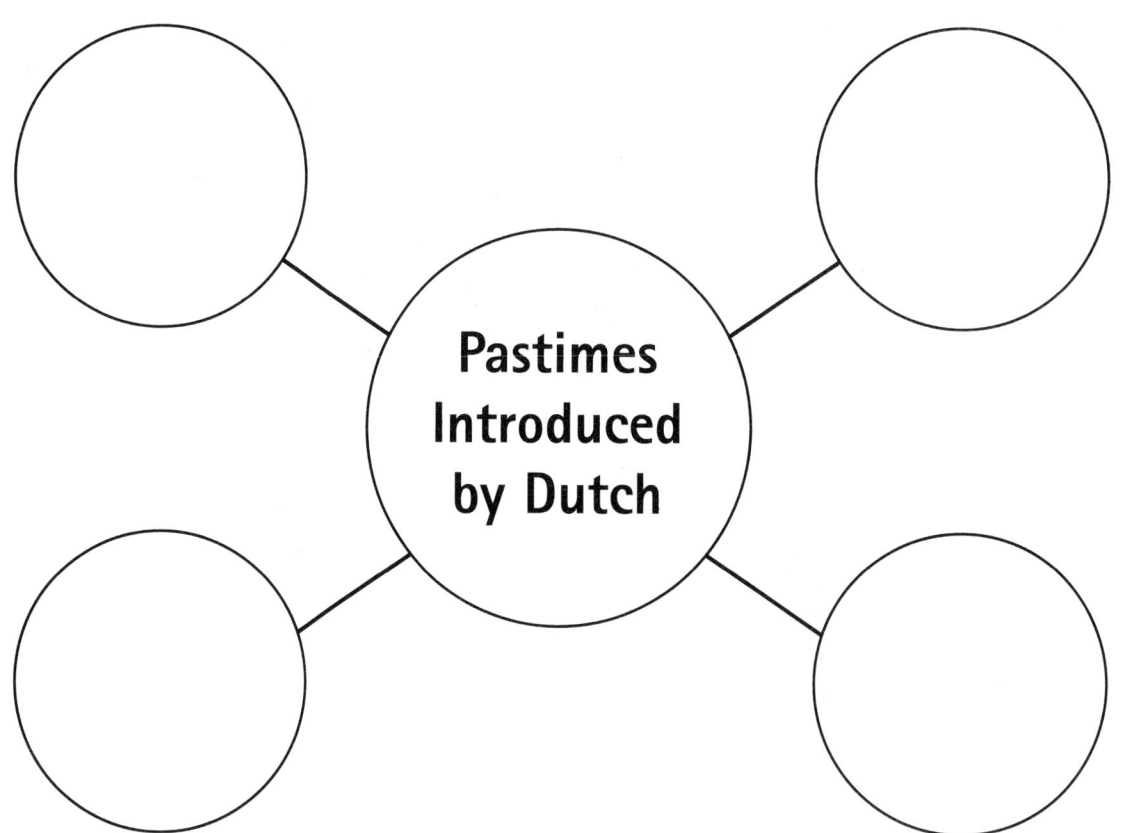

MORE! Find out who led the first Dutch settlers to North America. What was the name of the settlement he founded?

Slippery Slopes in the Seas

Icebergs can be slippery slopes for ships at sea. An iceberg can be dangerous to ships because more than 3/4 of it is under the water. Most of it isn't visible. Icebergs are found in the cold seas near the North and South Poles. The wind and currents move them through the water. As they move, icebergs often make creaking sounds. This sound has earned them the nickname of "growlers." Icebergs might be useful, too. Some scientists think these huge, freshwater chunks of ice could be towed to other places. Then the icebergs could be used to provide water to deserts.

Look at the topic in the web. Find details from the paragraph that tell about the topic. Write them in the web.

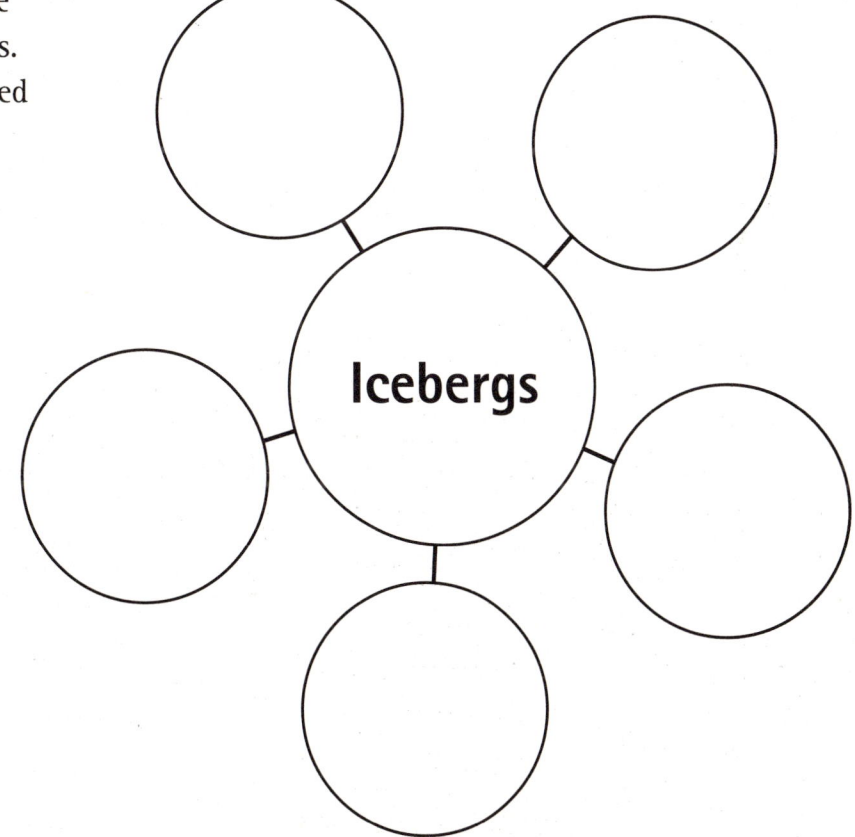

MORE! Find out what happened to the passenger ship *Titanic* in 1912.

Name _____   Date _____

July 4th Events

On July 4, 1776, Americans declared their nation's independence. This date is noteworthy to the United States for other reasons, too. President Calvin Coolidge was born on July 4th in 1872. The song "America" was first sung in public on July 4, 1832, in Boston, Massachusetts. The monument honoring George Washington was begun in Washington, D.C., on July 4, 1848. Perhaps most amazingly, Thomas Jefferson, who wrote the Declaration of Independence in 1776, died on July 4, 1826.

Decide what the main idea of the paragraph is. Write it in the center circle. Find details from the paragraph that tell about the topic. Write them in the web.

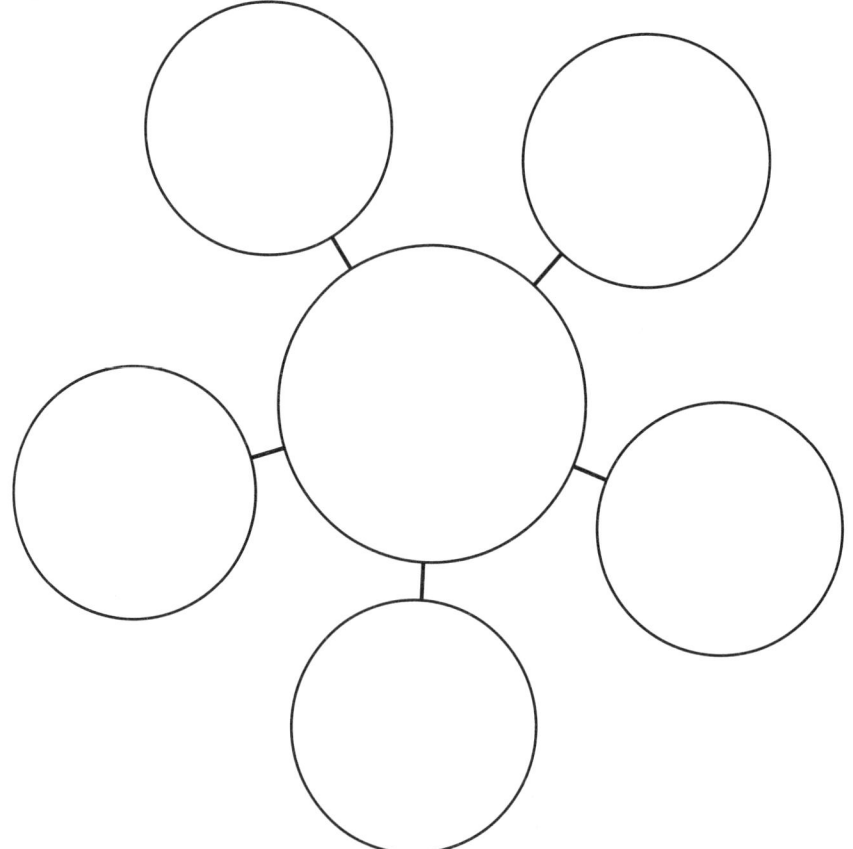

MORE! Find another fact about July 4th.

10

Name _____   Date _____

Get the Point

When you're scribbling a note with a pencil, do you ever wonder what this handy tool is made from? To get right to the point, a pencil is made of a number of materials. The inside is made of graphite that is reinforced with clay. Its wooden outside comes from cedar trees. The yellow paint on the wood is made from minerals, while the metal band at one end is aluminum. Should you make a mistake while writing, use the eraser. Its main materials are soybean oil and latex.

Decide what the main idea of the passage is. Write it in the center circle. Find details from the passage that tell about the topic. Write them in the web.

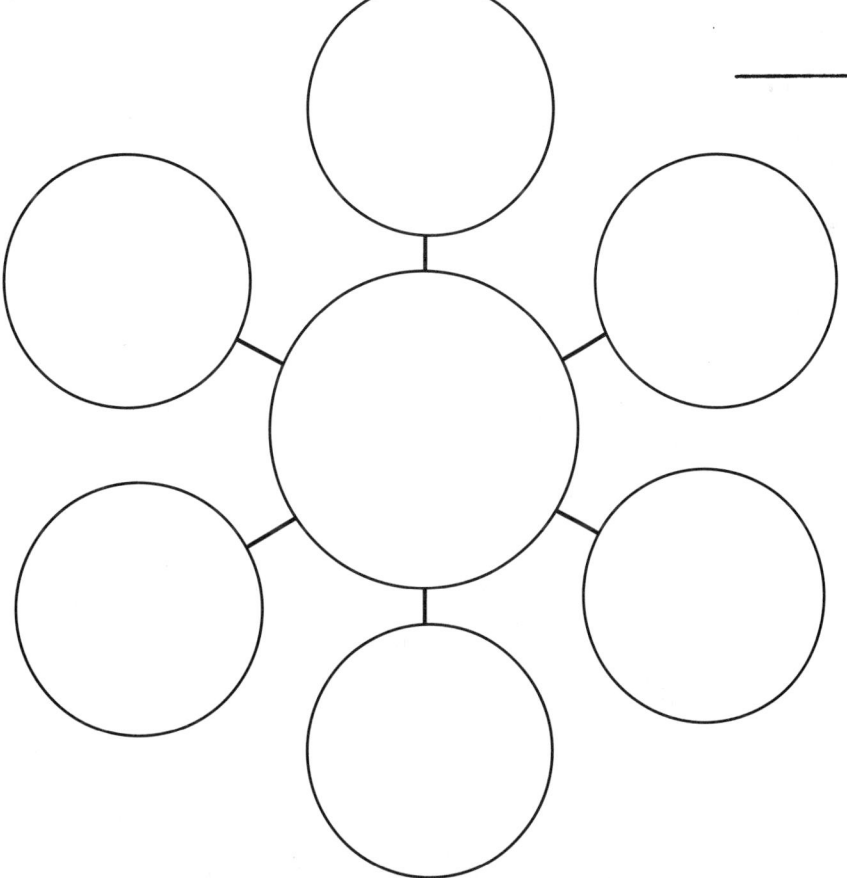

MORE! Use the information in the paragraph to make a diagram of a pencil. Write labels in your diagram.

Name _____   Date _____

Bird Words

How do towns get their names? Some names have been inspired by birds. Along the shores of Green Bay in Wisconsin, you'll find Egg Harbor. If you're in Oregon, you might visit Goose Creek. While in Massachusetts, you could stop at Buzzards Bay. Virginia has a town named Cuckoo, and Minnesota has one called Red Wing. Strangely enough, Bird City, Kansas, was not named for a feathered creature. This town was named for a man—Benjamin Bird, who was one of the first settlers in Kansas. Some people say that he was an "early Bird"!

Decide what the main idea of the paragraph is. Write it in the center circle. Find details from the paragraph that tell about the topic. Write them in the web.

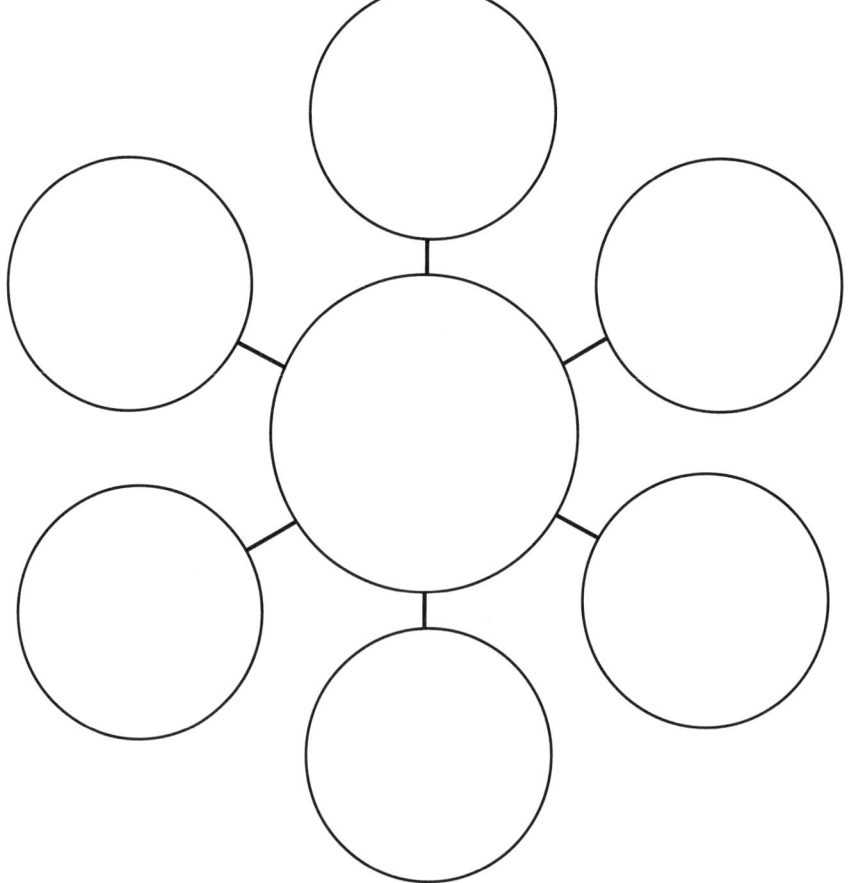

 **MORE!** A town in Pennsylvania is named Birdsboro. Find another town or city name to add to the web.

Name _____ Date _____

On the Radar Screen

You may have heard of radar, but do you know what the word means? *Radar* stands for "radio detection and ranging." Radar waves have many important uses in everyday life. Radar signals aid air traffic control in keeping track of planes. Burglar alarms use radar to detect the movements of intruders. Radar helps predict the weather. In baseball, radar measures the speed of pitches. Police use radar to detect drivers who are speeding. Radar even plays a role in the workings of microwave ovens.

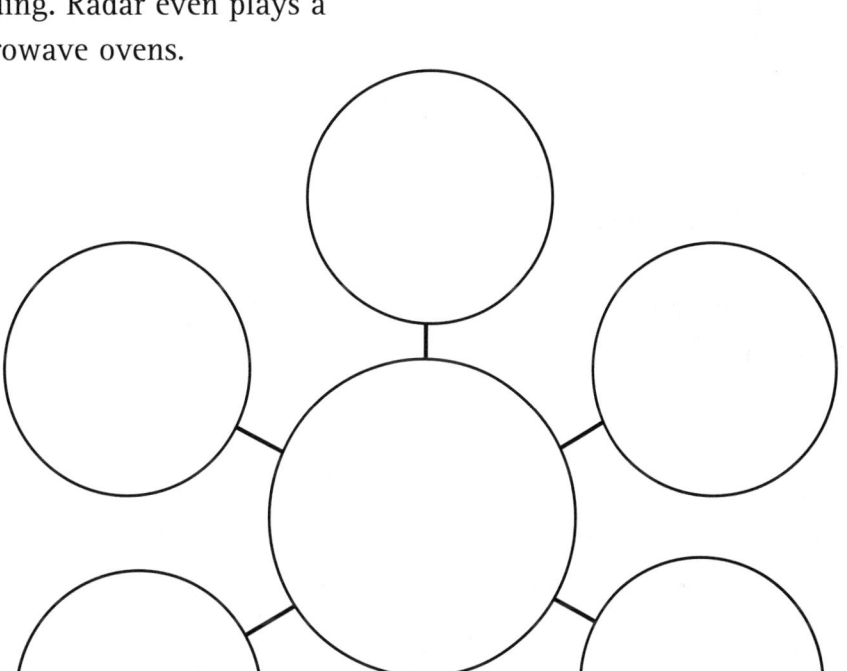

Decide what the main idea of the paragraph is. Write it in the center circle. Find details from the paragraph that tell about the topic. Write them in the web.

MORE! Use the web to tell someone how radar is used.

Name _____   Date _____

Food for Thought

Would you like another serving of potatoes? How much is a serving anyway? For people on diets, it's often hard to determine what a serving is. Luckily, a healthcare company has come up with guidelines that can help people visualize different serving sizes. For example, a medium potato is about the size of a computer mouse. Are you thinking of having a cup of fruit? Think about a baseball—it's about the right size. A cup of chopped vegetables equals a fist. A hockey puck is about the size of an average bagel. For three ounces of meat, visualize a bar of soap, but for three ounces of fish, imagine a checkbook!

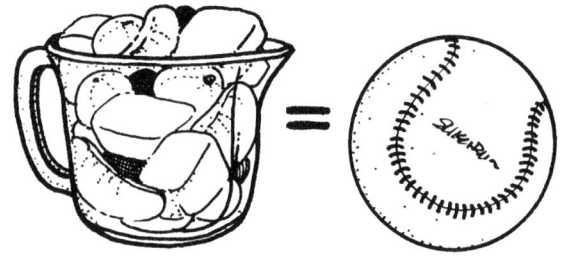

Decide what the main idea of the paragraph is. Write it in the center circle. Find details from the paragraph that tell about the topic. Write them in the web.

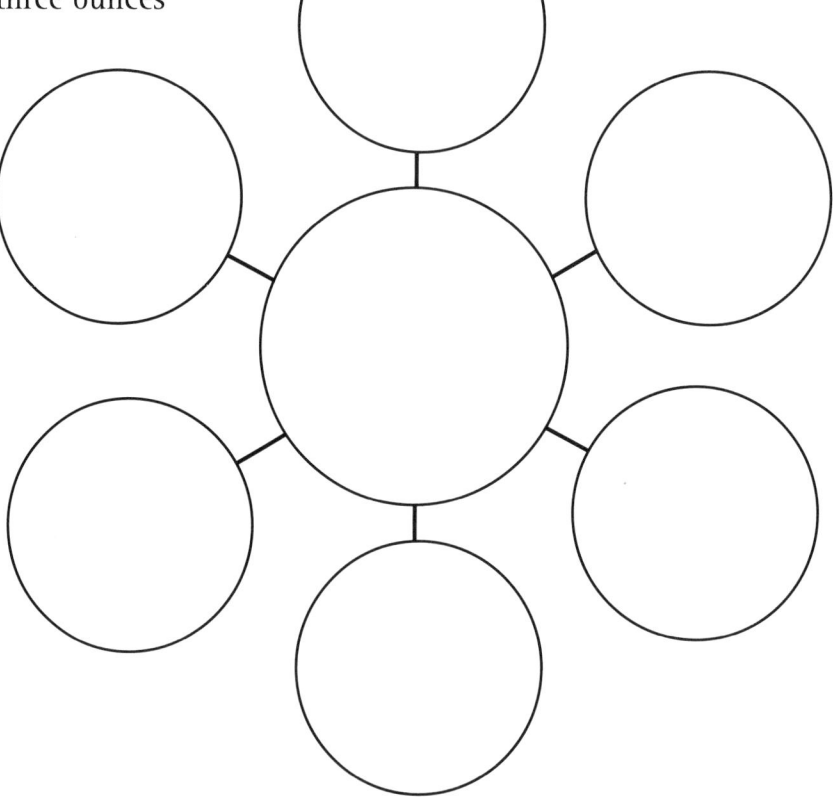

MORE! Think of your own visual examples of servings for these foods— 1/2 cup of rice, 2 ounces of cheese, and 1 cup of pasta.

Name _____   Date _____

Testing It Out

Use after completing Food for Thought on page 14.
Fill in the circle of the best answer.

1. The main idea of the passage is that people can use visual guidelines to—
- Ⓐ make their food taste better
- Ⓑ figure out the size of a serving of food
- Ⓒ believe in the success of their diet
- Ⓓ determine the best way to cook food

2. Visual guidelines for food servings were suggested by a—
- Ⓐ healthcare company
- Ⓑ hockey team
- Ⓒ group of dieters
- Ⓓ computer company

3. According to the guidelines, a cup of chopped vegetables is about the size of a—
- Ⓐ baseball
- Ⓑ hockey puck
- Ⓒ bagel
- Ⓓ fist

4. A computer mouse is about the size of—
- Ⓐ three ounces of fish
- Ⓑ a medium potato
- Ⓒ three ounces of meat
- Ⓓ a cup of fruit

5. You can guess that three ounces of meat—
- Ⓐ is about what someone on a diet should eat
- Ⓑ is more than what someone on a diet should eat
- Ⓒ tastes like a bar of soap
- Ⓓ tastes better than fish

6. To get the right portions without visual guidelines, you might need a—
- Ⓐ scale and bar of soap
- Ⓑ computer mouse and baseball
- Ⓒ measuring cup and checkbook
- Ⓓ scale and measuring cup

7. The visual guidelines assume that people know something about—
- Ⓐ sports and computers
- Ⓑ exercising to lose weight
- Ⓒ desserts without sugar
- Ⓓ healthcare companies

8. These guidelines would be most helpful to people who—
- Ⓐ learn by doing
- Ⓑ don't listen well
- Ⓒ think visually
- Ⓓ enjoy music

Name _____   Date _____

Musical Notes

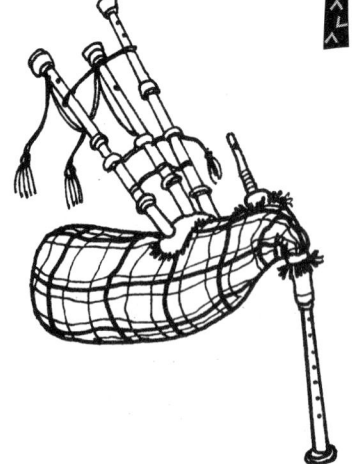

People have been making music with instruments for thousands of years. Some of the earliest music was made by people tapping sticks. Today people still use sticks to produce sounds on drums and xylophones. Many instruments make sounds when someone blows air into them. Some examples of these instruments include bagpipes, trumpets, and trombones. Other instruments have strings that a musician plucks or strokes. Guitars, lutes, sitars, and violins are string instruments.

Look at the topic and subtopic on the web. Add two more subtopics. Complete the web by writing details for each subtopic.

Topic → **Musical Instruments**

Subtopic → **Tapping Sticks**

Detail →

 Add one more instrument under each subtopic.

Name _____ Date _____

Let's Rock

Suppose you pick up a rock on a hike. What kind of rock could it be? It might be an igneous rock. This kind of rock is formed when hot liquid in the Earth cools and hardens. Basalt, pumice, and granite are igneous rocks. You might also have picked up a piece of sedimentary rock. Sedimentary rocks are made of layers of other rock. Limestone, sandstone, and chalk are examples of sedimentary rock. The third kind of rock is metamorphic. Marble and slate, two materials often used in buildings, are metamorphic rocks.

Look at the topic and subtopic on the web. Add two more subtopics. Complete the web by writing details for each subtopic.

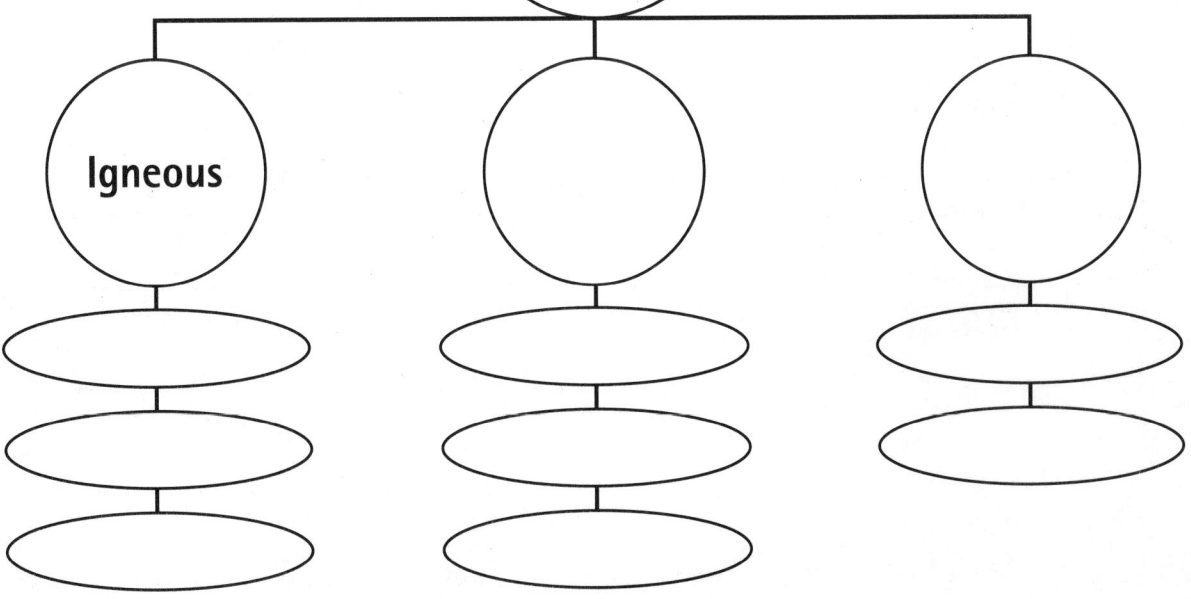

MORE! Add one more rock under each subtopic.

17

Name _____ Date _____

House Words

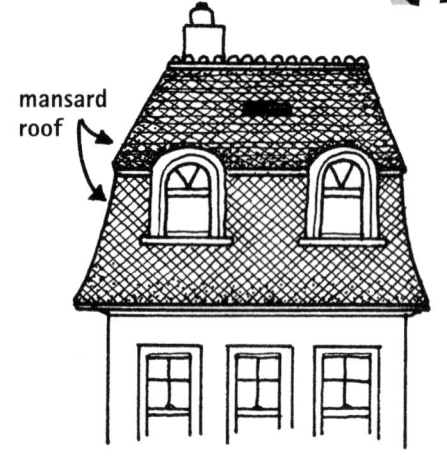

mansard roof

A house has a roof—but what kind of roof does it have? If the roof slopes on all sides, it's a hipped roof. If only two opposite sides slope, it's a gabled roof. The picture shows a mansard roof. Houses also have different kinds of windows and doors. Casement windows open on hinges. Sash windows slide up and down. French windows reach to the floor. A window in the roof is called a skylight. As for doors, you might come and go through a screen door, a sliding door, or a storm door.

Look at the topic and subtopic on the web. Add two more subtopics. Complete the web by writing details for each subtopic.

Houses

Roofs

MORE! Draw a picture of your own home. Label the parts.

Name _____ Date _____

Short For

You know that Mr. is short for mister, but do you know what CEO means? It stands for chief executive officer. Not all abbreviations stand for people. For example, Pk. means park, Rd. stands for road, and Mt. represents mountain. The abbreviation Dr. stands for two different words—doctor and drive. Units of measure also have abbreviations. Teaspoon is often shortened to tsp. and gal. stands for gallon.

Write the topic and three subtopics on the web. Complete the web by writing details for each subtopic.

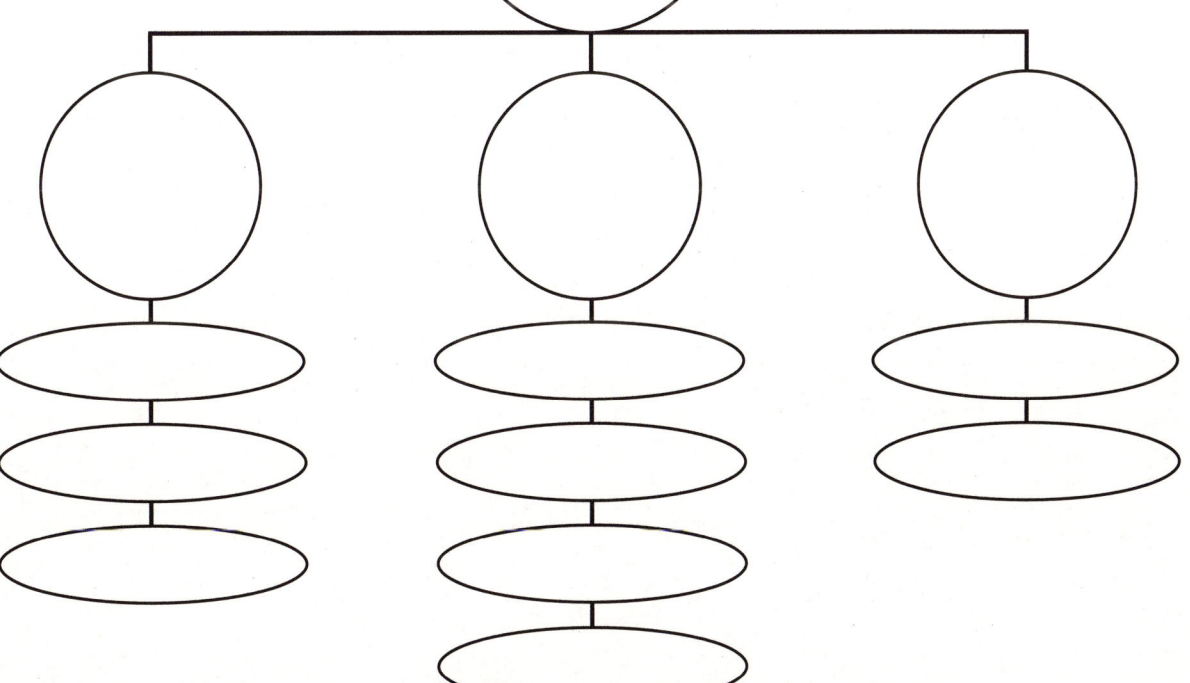

MORE! Write the abbreviations for the days of the week and the months of the year.

Name _____   Date _____

Counting Calories

Read the following riddle: What do you burn that doesn't catch fire?

What's the answer? Calories! When you exercise or do other activities, you burn calories. For example, you use up to 89 calories in 15 minutes when you run or do gymnastics. Activities such as sweeping, walking, or climbing stairs use 43 to 88 calories per quarter of an hour. Writing, watching television, and eating consume from 20 to 40 calories in fifteen minutes. Your present activity—reading—falls into the previous group as well.

Write the topic and three subtopics on the web. Complete the web by writing details for each subtopic.

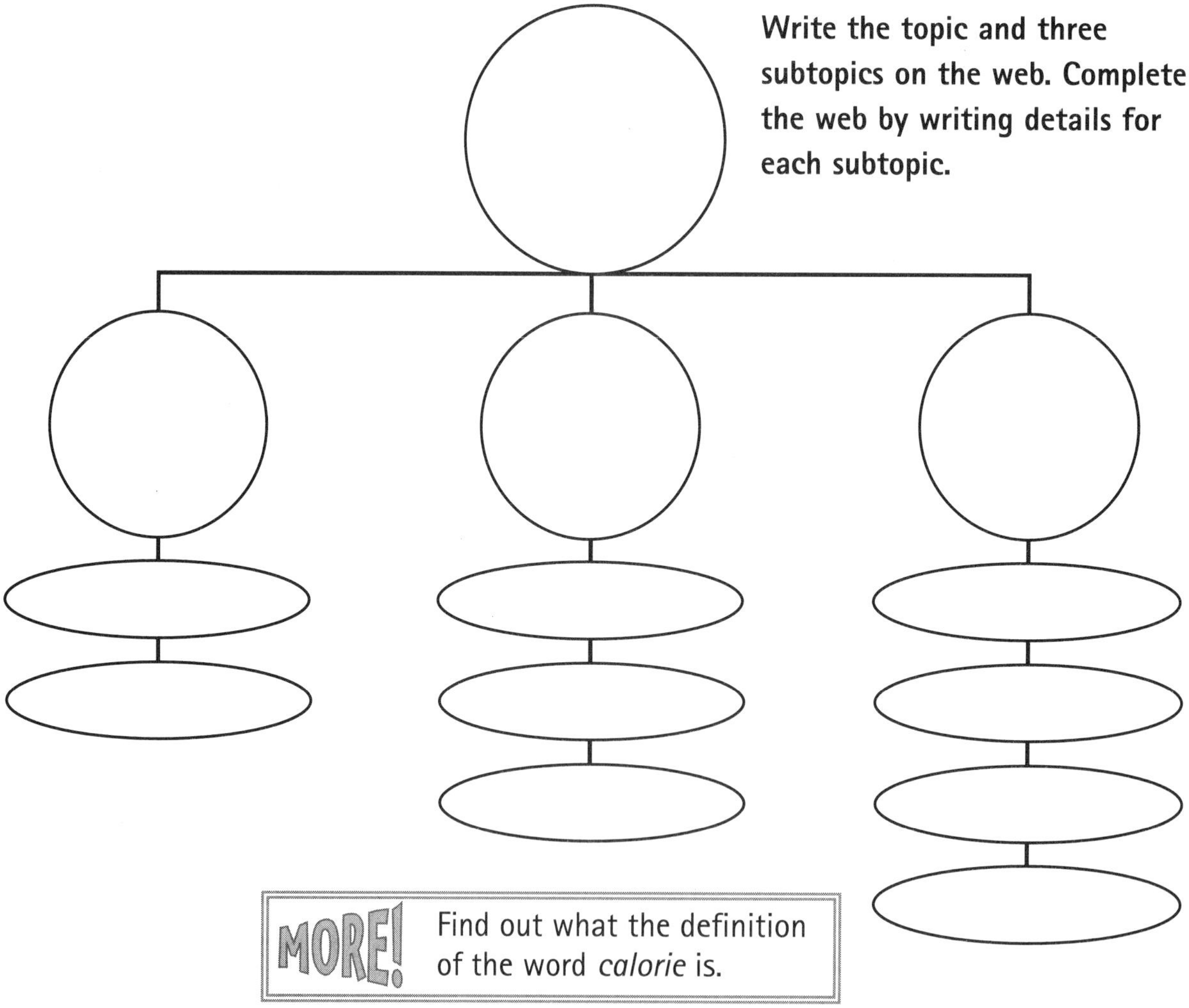

MORE! Find out what the definition of the word *calorie* is.

Preview of Prefixes

A prefix is a word part that always comes at the beginning of a word. When a prefix is added to a base word, it changes the word's meaning. The prefix *dis-* means "not." Think about how *dis-* affects the meaning of the words *disloyal, dishonest,* and *disagree.* One meaning for the prefix *re-* is "again." You see this prefix in words such as *redo, rebuild, reconsider,* and *renew.* The meaning of the prefix *over-* is "too much." Some examples of words containing this prefix are *overjoyed, oversleep, overflow,* and *overworked.*

Write the topic and three subtopics on the web. Complete the web by writing details for each subtopic.

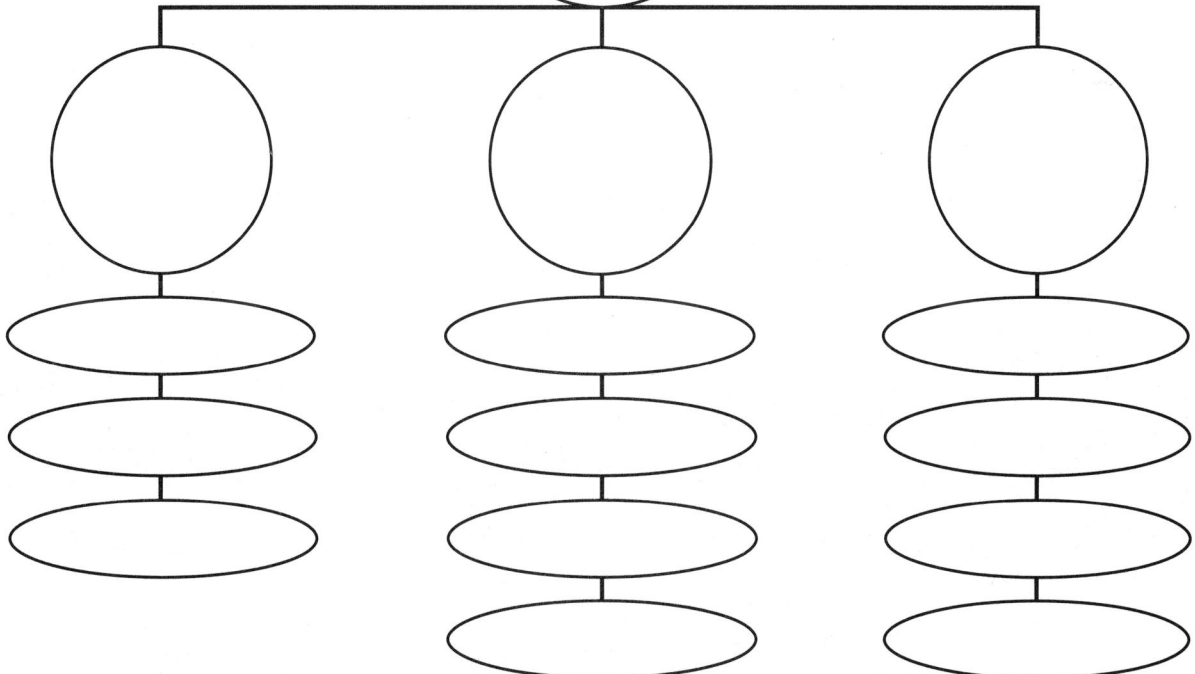

MORE! Find out the meaning of the prefixes *ex-, trans-,* and *inter-.*

Eating in Egypt

Suppose you lived thousands of years ago in Ancient Egypt. What would you have eaten? Like all Ancient Egyptians, you would eat bread with every meal. Garlic bread, raisin bread, and nutbread were three favorites. Egyptians also ate a lot of fruit including figs, dates, and pomegranates. Vegetables were also part of their diet. Lettuce, beans, onions, cucumbers, and leeks were all popular. How do you think you'd like your Egyptian meal?

Write the topic and three subtopics on the web. Complete the web by writing details for each subtopic.

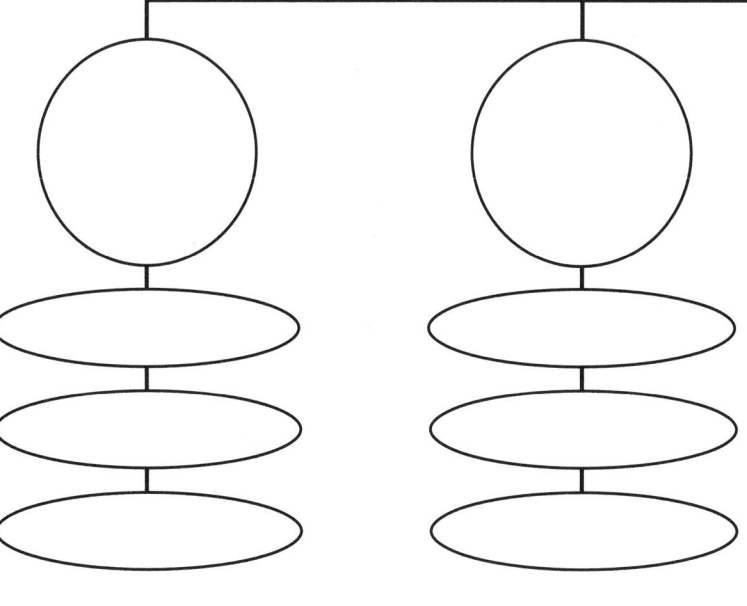

MORE! Write down everything you eat in one day.

Name _____   Date _____

Testing It Out

Use after completing Eating in Egypt on page 22.
Fill in the circle of the best answer.

1. One kind of food that Ancient Egyptians ate at every meal was—
   - Ⓐ lettuce
   - Ⓑ figs
   - Ⓒ bread
   - Ⓓ eggs

2. Ancient Egyptians often ate fruit called—
   - Ⓐ leeks
   - Ⓑ beans
   - Ⓒ apples
   - Ⓓ dates

3. A food group that includes onions is—
   - Ⓐ grains
   - Ⓑ meat
   - Ⓒ vegetables
   - Ⓓ cheese

4. Because Ancient Egyptians made raisin bread, you can guess they grew—
   - Ⓐ grapes
   - Ⓑ bread
   - Ⓒ pomegranates
   - Ⓓ cucumbers

5. From this passage, you can guess that Ancient Egyptians—
   - Ⓐ hunted animals
   - Ⓑ grew crops
   - Ⓒ raised chickens
   - Ⓓ fished in the sea

6. One kind of tree that most likely grew in Egypt was the—
   - Ⓐ fig tree
   - Ⓑ bean tree
   - Ⓒ oak tree
   - Ⓓ pine tree

7. Because they had fruit, you can guess that Ancient Egyptians probably—
   - Ⓐ raised bees
   - Ⓑ drank juices
   - Ⓒ drank milk
   - Ⓓ ate potatoes

8. A food that the passage does not mention is—
   - Ⓐ vegetables
   - Ⓑ nuts
   - Ⓒ fruit
   - Ⓓ meat

Name _____ Date _____

Best Books

In 1936, the winner was *Caddie Woodlawn* by Carol Ryrie Brink. In 1961, the winner was *Island of the Blue Dolphins* by Scott O'Dell. Each of these books won the Newbery Medal, an award given every year for the most distinguished contribution to children's literature. Have you ever read Ellen Raskin's *The Westing Game*? It won the Newbery Medal in 1979. Beverly Cleary's *Dear Mr. Henshaw* won in 1984. A more recent winner, *Bud, Not Buddy* by Christopher Paul Curtis, received the Newbery Medal in 2000. An award-winning book that is still popular today, *The Voyages of Dr. Dolittle* by Hugh Lofting, was the second Newbery recipient in 1923.

Add the book titles in the correct order to the time line. The first one is done for you.

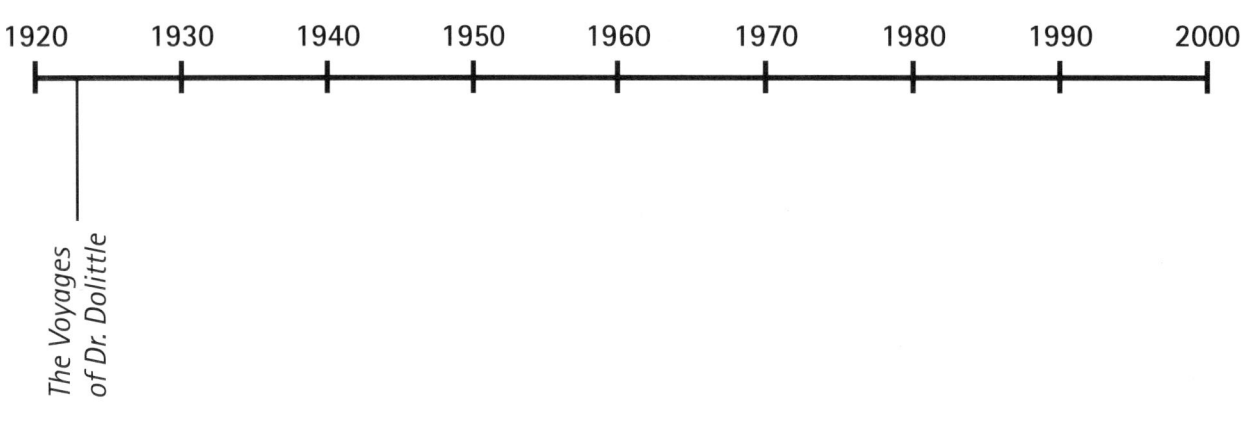

 Read a Newbery Award book.

Colorful Events

History is full of colorful events. Television first appeared in living color in 1953. People began taking color photographs in 1935. Colorful music history was made in 1970 when a frog puppet named Kermit croaked out the song "Bein' Green." The year 1968 marked a milestone in another hue with the release of the movie *The Yellow Submarine* starring the Beatles. Traffic signals appeared in 1920. Another colorful event occurred in 1927 when bathtubs and sinks—once only available in white—were sold in tones such as Spring Green, Autumn Brown, and Horizon Blue for the first time.

Add six events in the correct place to the time line. The first event is done for you.

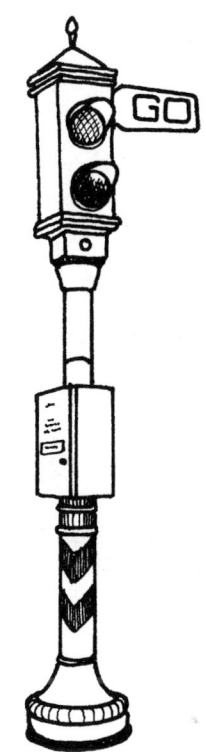

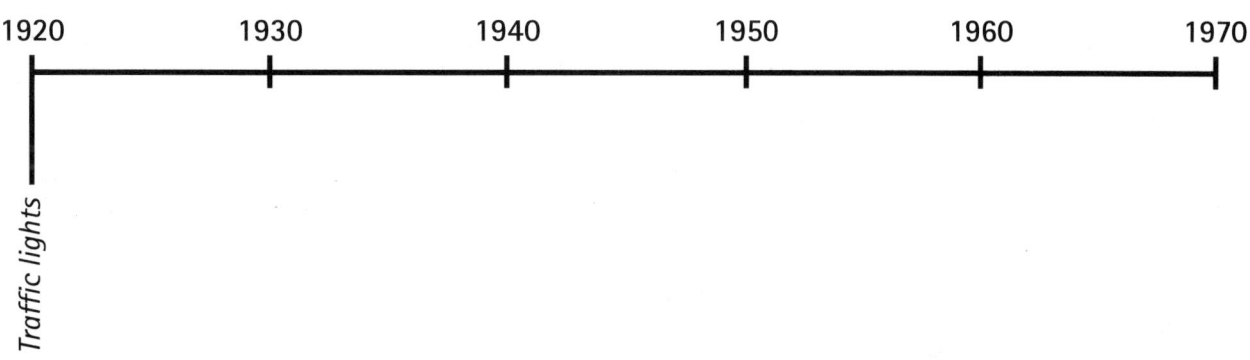

MORE! Add another color-related event to the time line.

Trees of History

Some trees really stand the test of time. George Washington planted trees on his farm at Mount Vernon, Virginia, in 1785. The tulip poplars that he planted are still growing today. A honey locust tree stands near the military cemetery in Gettysburg, Pennsylvania. It was there when Abraham Lincoln gave his famous address in 1863. Hikers on nature trails in Walden Woods in Massachusetts see the same red maples that Henry David Thoreau wrote about in 1843. Since 1912, beautiful cherry trees from Japan have bloomed each spring in Washington, D.C. At Council Bluffs, Iowa, black locust trees planted in 1823 still honor the explorers Lewis and Clark.

Write the five events in the correct place on the time line.

1780   1800   1820   1840   1860   1880   1900   1920

MORE! Find the places mentioned in the passage on a map.

Many Milestones

People have been driving cars for more than a century. If you traveled back in time, you'd find some interesting auto facts along the way. In 1901, car drivers in New York City had to have their initials on their cars. The first license plates were issued two years later in Massachusetts. Cars got electric headlights in 1912, and the first white sidewall tires appeared in 1918. The first auto theft was reported in St. Louis in 1905. In 1911, the first 500-mile race took place in Indianapolis. Parking meters first appeared in 1935 in Oklahoma City.

Write the seven events in the correct order on the time line.

1900   1905   1910   1915   1920   1925   1930   1935

MORE! In 1913, for the first time, more cars than horse buggies were manufactured. Add this fact to the time line.

Name _____ Date _____

Time for Sports

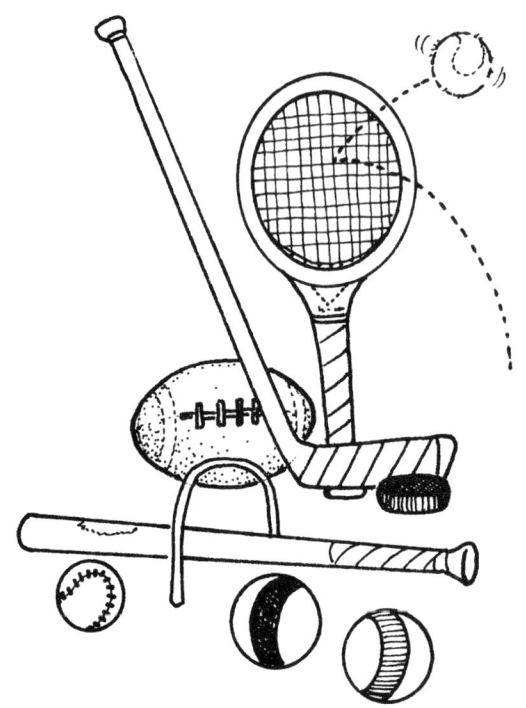

The 1800s were important years for sports in the United States. Not only was basketball invented in 1891, but ice hockey was also introduced from Canada in 1893. Earlier in the century, Americans began playing croquet, which was imported from England in 1860. Lawn tennis, a game played in Bermuda, came to this country in 1874. The first bicycles in the United States were made here in 1878. An American invented roller skates in 1863. The first baseball club was organized in 1845, while the first college football game was played in 1861.

Write eight events on the time line in the correct order.

1840   1850   1860   1870   1880   1890   1900

MORE! Choose one sport. Find out more about its early days in the United States.

Jersey Firsts

New Jersey was one of the first states in the nation. The state has had many other firsts since then. For example, the first submarine was built there in 1878. New Jersey also had the first organized baseball game in 1846, the first ferry service in 1811, the first yacht club in 1884, and the first boardwalk in 1870. Thanks to Thomas Edison and his inventions, the state has also scored the following firsts: the first phonograph in 1877, the first motion picture in 1889, and the first incandescent lamp in 1879.

Write eight events on the time line in the correct order.

1810 1820 1830 1840 1850 1860 1870 1880 1890

 Find another fact about New Jersey.

Name _____ Date _____

Presidential Passages

George Washington, the first President of the United States, took office in 1789. The first president to live in the White House, however, was John Adams. He and his wife Abigail moved there in 1800. Since then, technology has changed the lives of presidents. In 1833, Andrew Jackson was the first president to ride on a train. James Polk was the first president to be photographed in 1849. Benjamin Harrison was the first president to have electricity in the White House in 1891.

Presidential firsts also relate to advances in communications. In 1993, William Clinton was the first president to have e-mail in the White House. In 1955, Dwight Eisenhower was the first president to appear on color TV. The first president to make a radio broadcast from the White House was Calvin Coolidge in 1925.

Write eight events on the time line in the correct order.

1750   1800   1850   1900   1950   2000

| MORE! | Discover which president was the first to ride on a steamboat, in a car, and on an airplane. |

Name _____ Date _____

Testing It Out

Use after completing Presidential Passages on page 30.
Fill in the circle of the best answer.

1. The first presidential radio broadcast from the White House occurred—
   - Ⓐ after Eisenhower was on TV
   - Ⓑ during Coolidge's term
   - Ⓒ before Jackson became president
   - Ⓓ in the nineteenth century

2. The first presidential photo was taken in—
   - Ⓐ 1891
   - Ⓑ 1800
   - Ⓒ 1833
   - Ⓓ 1849

3. From the passage, you can guess that before 1891, presidents—
   - Ⓐ used gas lamps for light
   - Ⓑ rode in automobiles
   - Ⓒ used fluorescent lights
   - Ⓓ did not have running water

4. You can guess that photography was—
   - Ⓐ not invented until the 1900s
   - Ⓑ forbidden in Washington's time
   - Ⓒ invented in the 1800s
   - Ⓓ invented by James Polk

5. You can infer that President James Polk never knew about—
   - Ⓐ railroads
   - Ⓑ the White House
   - Ⓒ photography
   - Ⓓ computers

6. President Harrison would be surprised to learn about the development of—
   - Ⓐ photography
   - Ⓑ television
   - Ⓒ electricity
   - Ⓓ railroads

7. George Washington was president for eight years so you can figure out that the second president was—
   - Ⓐ William Clinton
   - Ⓑ James Polk
   - Ⓒ John Adams
   - Ⓓ Andrew Jackson

8. The president who probably benefited the least from technology was—
   - Ⓐ Benjamin Harrison
   - Ⓑ William Clinton
   - Ⓒ Calvin Coolidge
   - Ⓓ George Washington

Name _____   Date _____

Double Dakota

Both North and South Dakota are midwestern states on the Great Plains. If you visit Bismarck, you'll be in the capital of North Dakota. South Dakota's capital is Pierre. While in South Dakota, you might travel through the Black Hills. The faces of four presidents—George Washington, Thomas Jefferson, Abraham Lincoln, and Theodore Roosevelt—are carved into Mt. Rushmore there. Other interesting South Dakota sights are the dry landscape of Badlands National Park and bison roaming in Custer State Park. In North Dakota, you might visit the International Peace Garden on the Canadian border.

Find facts in the passage about North and South Dakota. Write the facts under the correct headings on the Venn diagram. Under "Both," write facts that are true of both states.

North Dakota   **South Dakota**

Both

Bismark is capital.   midwestern states   Pierre is capital.

MORE! Locate North and South Dakota on a U.S. map.

Name _____ Date _____

Into the Woods

If a tree stays green all year and bears cones instead of flowers, it is a conifer. In general, conifers grow best in cool, dry conditions. There are two types of coniferous forests—temperate and boreal. Temperate forests grow in mild climates and are often found along coastlines. The giant sequoia trees grow in temperate forests. Boreal forests include pine, spruce, hemlock, and fir trees. You'll find boreal forests in northern regions where summers are short and winters are long.

Find facts in the passage about temperate and boreal forests. Write the facts under the correct headings on the Venn diagram. Under "Both," write facts that are true of both kinds of forests.

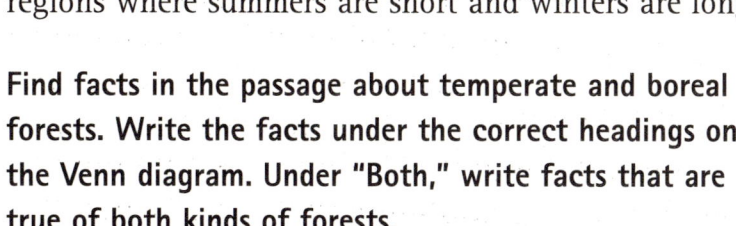

Temperate — giant sequoia

Both — coniferous

Boreal — pine

MORE! Find out the names of two other kinds of forests. What kinds of trees grow in them?

33

Name _____   Date _____

Catch This

Baseball catchers still stand behind home plate, but their equipment has changed during the last century. In 1900, a catcher's mask had a solid steel grill that was padded with doe skin. Today's catcher wears an ultra-light mask made of hollow wire with a deer skin covering. Modern catchers also wear helmets made from high-impact plastic. Catchers in 1900 had no leg guards. Catchers today wear specially fitted shin guards with padded kneecaps. Although catchers have worn gloves for the past 100 years, the early gloves were bulky and pillow-like. The gloves of today are molded to the hand. Chest protectors in 1900 were heavy leather or canvas pads; now they are lighter and made of form-fitting foam.

Write three headings on the Venn diagram.
Under each heading, add facts from the passage.

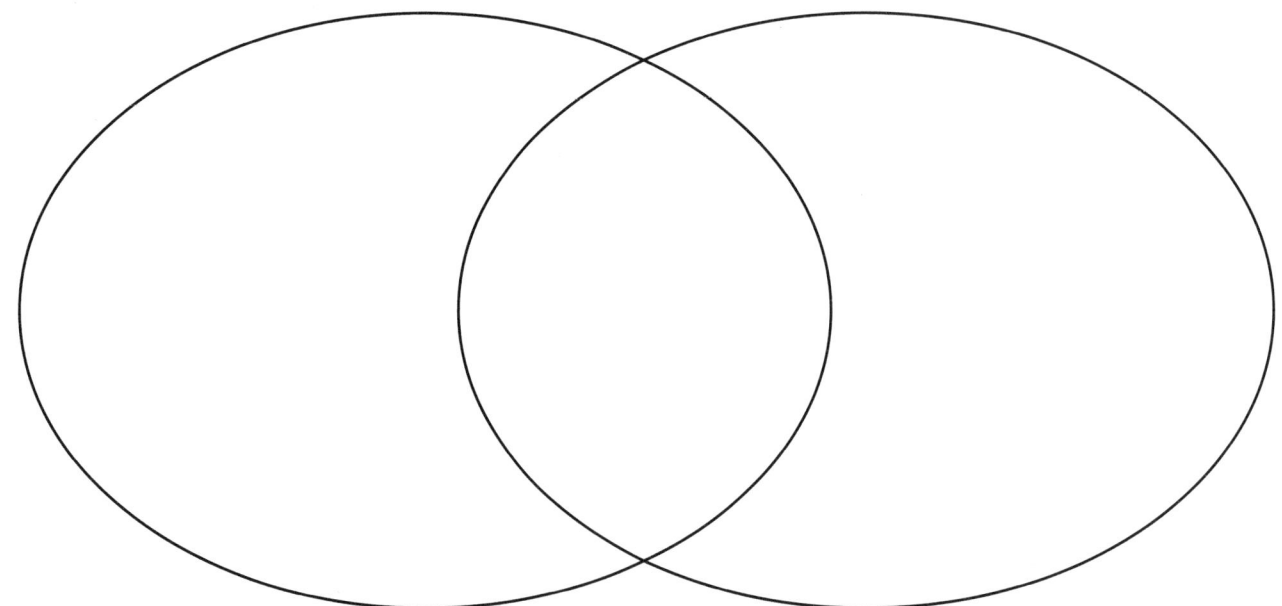

MORE! What is another difference in baseball between 1900 and 2000? Report your fact to the class.

Name _____   Date _____

Temperature Tales

When it's 60° Centigrade, it's 140° Fahrenheit. People use both ways to measure the temperature. The Fahrenheit thermometer is named after German physicist, Gabriel Daniel Fahrenheit. He invented this thermometer in the early 1700s. On this scale, water freezes at 32°F and boils at 212°F. The Celsius scale was created by Swedish astronomer Anders Celsius in 1742. On the Celsius scale, also called the centigrade scale, the freezing point of water is 0°C and its boiling point is 100°C. Although most countries use the Celsius thermometer, the United States measures temperature with the Fahrenheit scale.

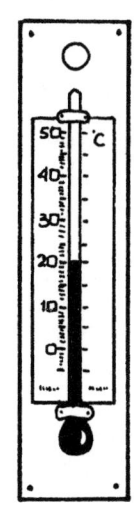

Write three headings on the Venn diagram. Under each heading, add facts from the passage.

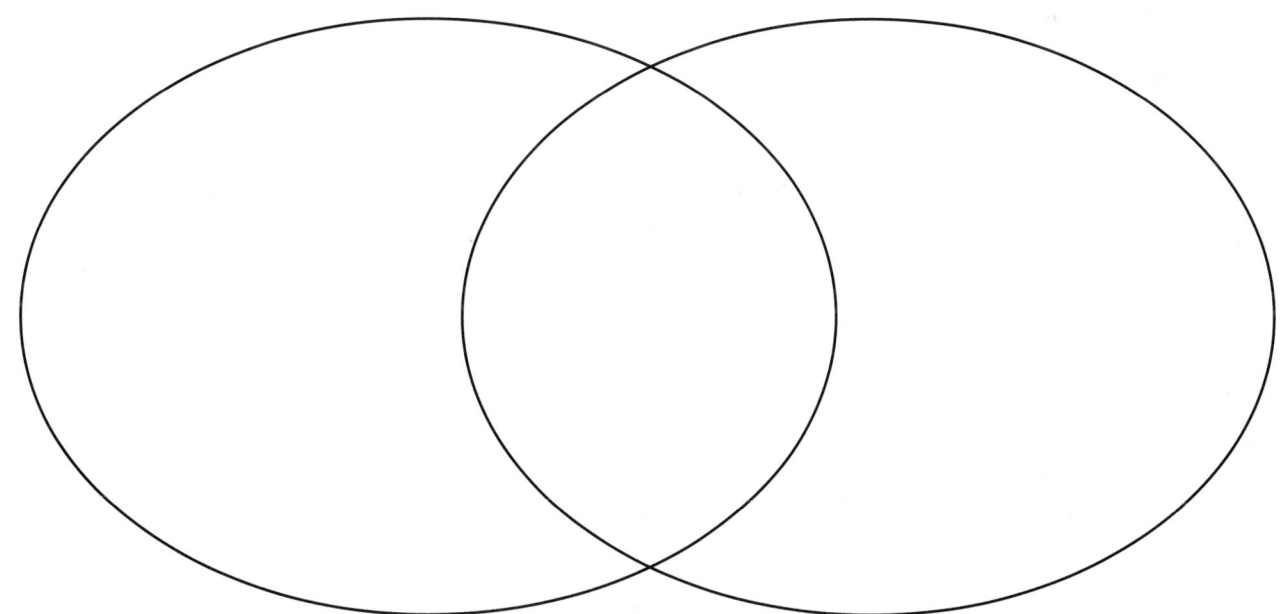

MORE! To convert Fahrenheit to Celsius, subtract 32 degrees from the Fahrenheit temperature. Multiply the difference by 5/9. Find the Celsius temperature for 50°F.

Name _____ Date _____

Venus Visit

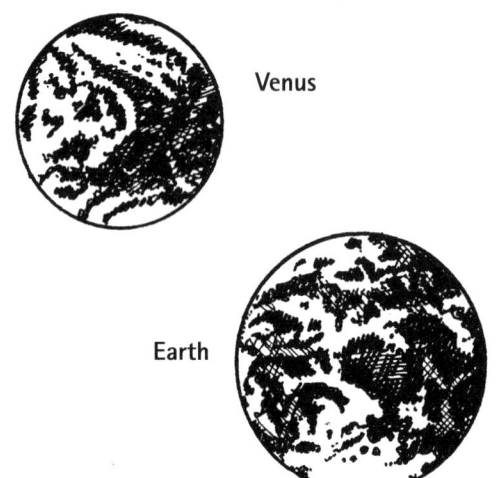

Venus

Earth

How would you like to spend a day on the neighboring planet of Venus? A day on Venus would be much longer than 24 hours. It would last for more than 116 Earth days! You'd also have to be able to breathe carbon dioxide instead of oxygen. You'd be nearer to the sun than you are on Earth. But you wouldn't see a moon because Venus doesn't have one. Are Earth and Venus alike in any way? Both planets are made of rock, and neither has rings like Jupiter and Saturn do.

Write three headings on the Venn diagram. Under each heading, add facts from the passage.

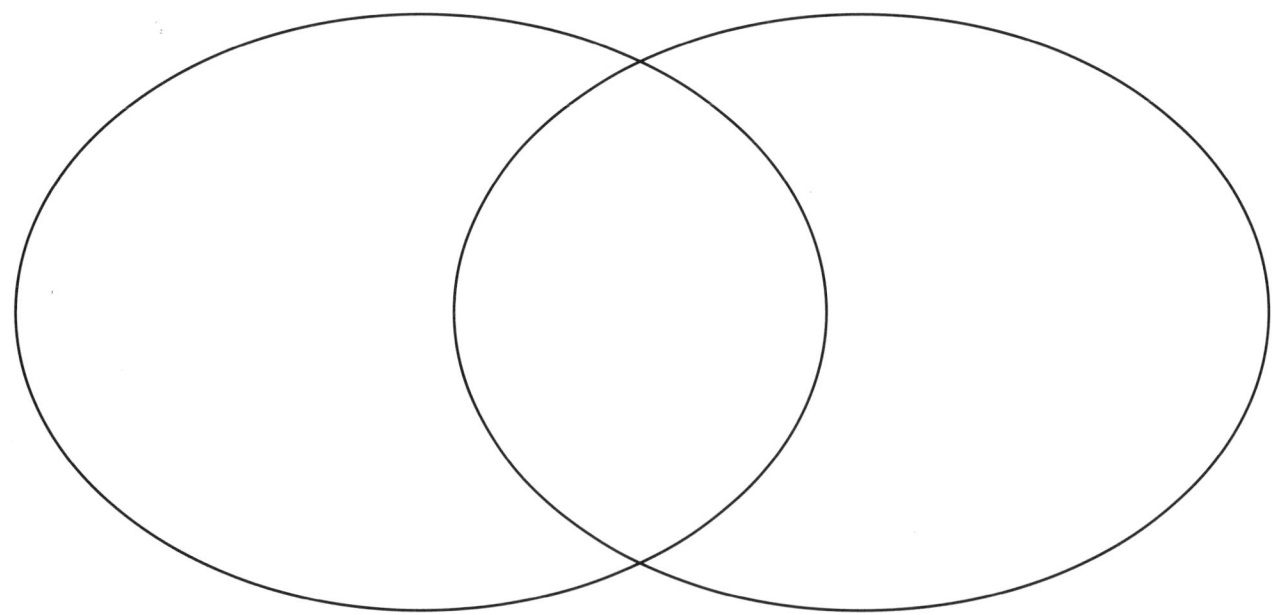

MORE! Compare Earth to one of the other planets.

Name _____   Date _____

Out in Front

To a weather forecaster, a front is the boundary of a mass of warm or cold air. A warm front occurs when warm air moves toward an area of cold air. The warm air, which is lighter, slides over the heavier cold air. The result is that clouds form and rain or other precipitation usually falls. When cold air moves in on a mass of warm air, scientists call it a cold front. As you can guess, the heavier cold air slides under the warm air and pushes it up. Again, clouds form as a result. In this case, thunderstorms may occur.

Write three headings on the Venn diagram. Under each heading, add facts from the passage.

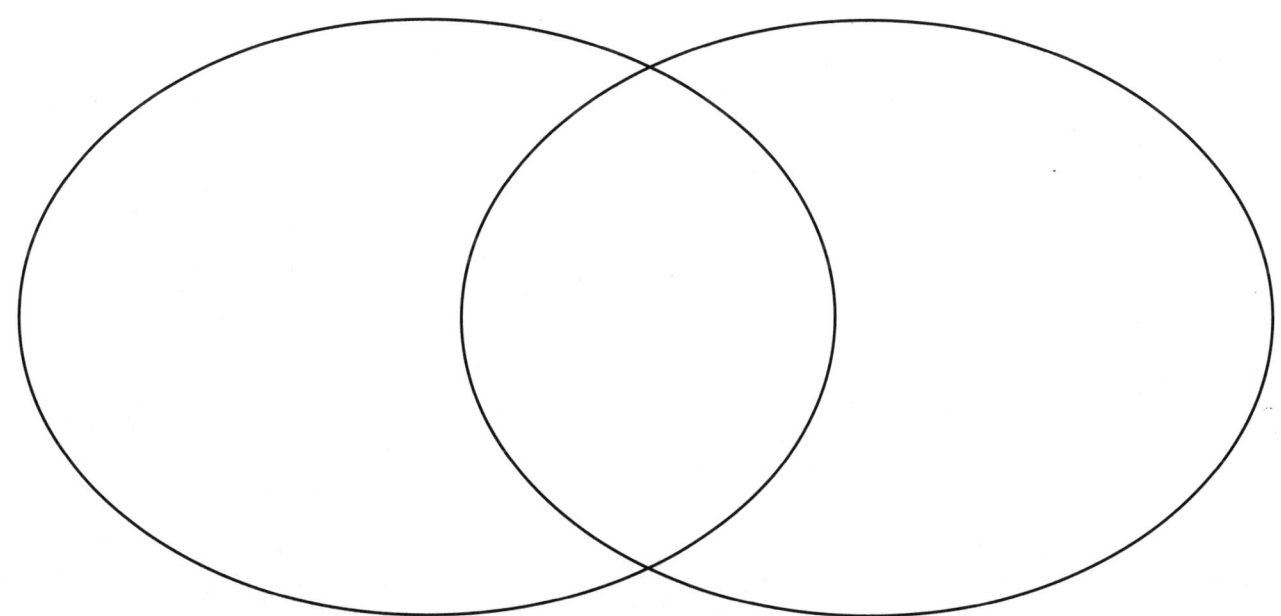

MORE! Give a radio or television weather forecast describing what will happen when either kind of front moves in.

Many Thanks

Giving thanks is a custom among people all around the world. Like the American Thanksgiving, many celebrations began as a way of showing gratitude for a good harvest. In Korea, people have celebrated a fall holiday called Ch'usok for more than 1,000 years. Families prepare special foods using newly harvested crops. On the holiday itself, Koreans remember their ancestors. Later in the day, they enjoy a feast of rice cakes, fresh fruit, and vegetable soup. In the United States, Thanksgiving honors a tradition that began in 1621 with the Pilgrims and the Wampanoag Indians. A typical American Thanksgiving includes foods such as turkey, potatoes, cranberries, stuffing, vegetables, and pumpkin pie. Families and friends give thanks not only for their meal, but also for the freedoms they enjoy as Americans.

Write three headings on the diagram. Under each heading, add facts from the passage.

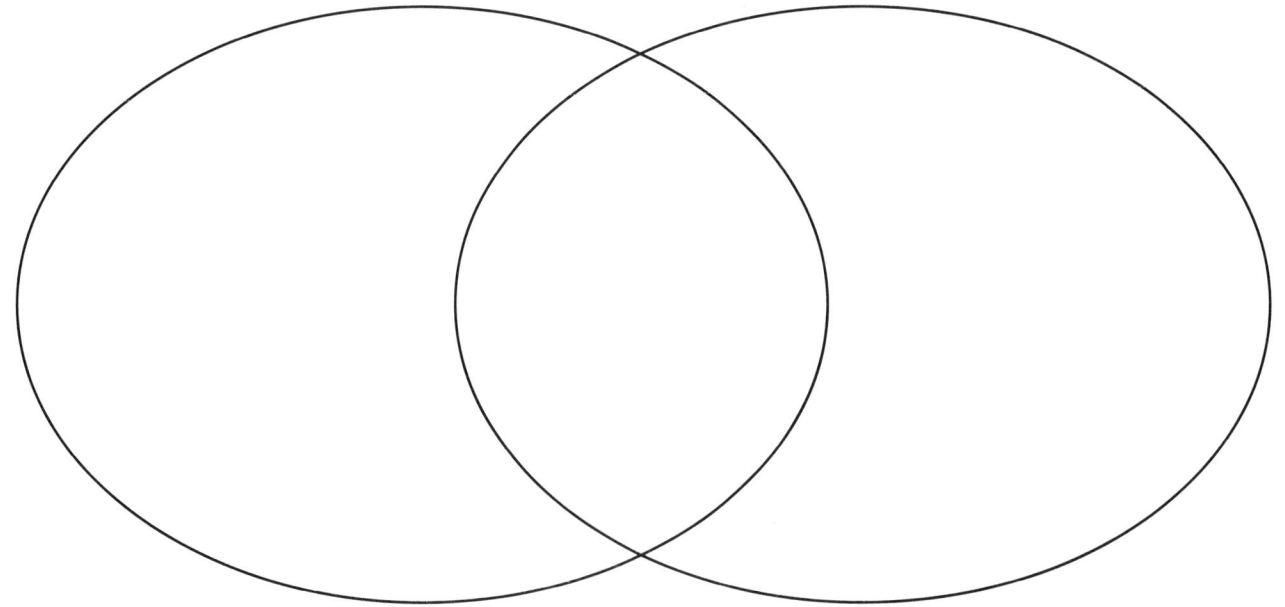

MORE! Find out who Sarah Josepha Hall was and why she is known in the U.S. as "the mother of Thanksgiving."

Name _____ Date _____

Testing It Out

Use after completing Many Thanks on page 38.
Fill in the circle of the best answer.

1. The passage compares—
   - Ⓐ Americans and Pilgrims
   - Ⓑ kinds of memorial services
   - Ⓒ Ch'usok and Thanksgiving
   - Ⓓ Wampanoags and Koreans

2. On both holidays, people—
   - Ⓐ give gifts
   - Ⓑ make rice cakes
   - Ⓒ roast turkeys
   - Ⓓ show gratitude

3. Both holidays are celebrated—
   - Ⓐ in the spring
   - Ⓑ before the harvest
   - Ⓒ in the fall
   - Ⓓ around the world

4. The Korean holiday—
   - Ⓐ is about the freedoms of Korea
   - Ⓑ is also about ancestor worship
   - Ⓒ began in 1621
   - Ⓓ is more recent than the American holiday

5. A traditional food on Thanksgiving in the U.S. is—
   - Ⓐ rice cakes
   - Ⓑ cranberries
   - Ⓒ fresh fruit
   - Ⓓ hot soup

6. A food that people do <u>not</u> usually eat on Ch'usok is—
   - Ⓐ fruit
   - Ⓑ vegetables
   - Ⓒ rice
   - Ⓓ turkey

7. The people celebrating together at both holidays are usually—
   - Ⓐ family members
   - Ⓑ Americans
   - Ⓒ Pilgrims
   - Ⓓ Koreans

8. From this passage you can guess that—
   - Ⓐ Koreans do not eat dessert
   - Ⓑ rice is an important food in Korea
   - Ⓒ all Thanksgivings are the same
   - Ⓓ Americans do not eat rice

Name _____ Date _____

The Elves of Iceland

If you visited Iceland, would you look for elves? Many people in Iceland believe in elves and other magical folk that can cause mischief. Some Icelanders consult a person called an elf-spotter before building a home. The elf-spotter ensures that the land is elf free. The country's Public Roads Administration has been known to reroute highways because of angry elves. Some Icelandic tourist groups have even made maps charting elf haunts for curious visitors!

Read the cause and one of its effects on the map. Find two other effects in the passage. Write them on the map.

Effects

| People consult elf-spotters before building homes. |

Cause

| Icelanders believe in elves. | →

 Locate Iceland on a globe or world map.

Name _____ Date _____

Address Unknown

Addresses—street names and house numbers—don't exist in Saipan. Nobody on this tropical island in the Pacific Ocean has an address. As a result, there is no mail delivery. Instead, people go to the central post office to get their letters and packages. When islanders give directions to get someplace, they refer to landmarks, such as a funny-looking tree or bumps in the road. When someone in Saipan orders pizza, it can take a long time for it to be delivered!

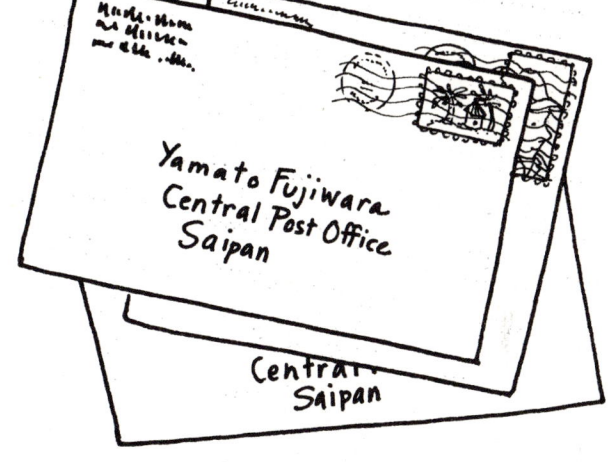

Read the cause on the map. Find three effects in the passage. Write them on the map.

Cause

| Addresses don't exist in Saipan. |

→

Effects

| |
| |
| |

MORE! Think of at least two reasons why someone might like <u>not</u> having an address.

Name _____ Date _____

Moonwalkers on City Streets

Do you need some exercise? Do you want to see some city sights? Perhaps you want to assert your rights as a pedestrian in a city designed for cars. Then you might want to join a group called Moonwalkers in Bethlehem, Pennsylvania. The Moonwalkers meet once a week at night. Then they stride through their city, up hills, down streets, over bridges, and along canals. What are some other reasons that people enjoy moonwalking? They get to meet other members of their community, and they enjoy being out at night.

Find five causes and one effect in the passage. Write them on the map.

Causes **Effect**

MORE! Make a list of five synonyms for the word *walk*. Use each word in a sentence.

    42

Name _____ Date _____

The Real McCoy

In 1872, Elijah McCoy, an engineer from Canada, invented a way to keep the moving parts of train cars constantly oiled. As a result, trains did not have to stop every few miles for oiling. Soon, no machine was considered any good unless it had one of McCoy's oil cups. To be sure they got a good locomotive, engineers began saying they wanted "the real McCoy." In time, this phrase came to mean "the real thing."

Find a cause and a chain of four effects in the passage. Write them on the map.

Cause **Effects**

☐ → ☐ → ☐ → ☐ → ☐

Read *The Real McCoy* by Wendy Towle.

Name _____ Date _____

A Cold Fish

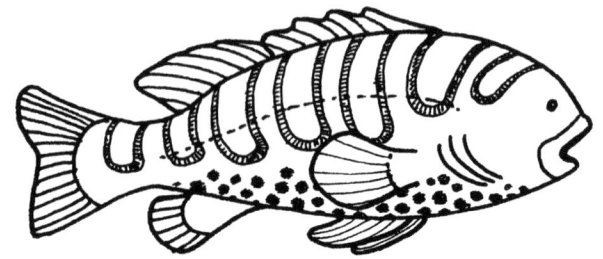

It was the winter of 1912. Clarence Birdseye went ice-fishing on a day when the temperature was 20 degrees below zero. *Brrrr!* As Birdseye pulled a fish from the lake, it quickly froze. Back at his camp, Birdseye tossed the frozen fish into water. Much to his surprise, the fish began to swim. Birdseye then tried preserving other foods by freezing them quickly. In 1925, he started the Birdseye Company. The company produced frozen foods—of course.

Find a cause and a chain of four effects in the passage. Write them on the map.

Cause   **Effects**

☐ → ☐ → ☐ → ☐ → ☐

MORE! Look up the definition of the word *serendipity* in a dictionary. What was serendipitous about Birdseye's discovery?

Name _____ Date _____

Plans, Please

Pierre L'Enfant, who designed the city of Washington, D.C., was a difficult man. He would only show his plans for the new city to his two assistants. As a result, L'Enfant was fired. He was so furious that he took his plans and returned to his home in France. The Americans were very upset. How could they complete the capital? Luckily, Benjamin Banneker, one of L'Enfant's assistants, had memorized the plans. He was able to redraw them. Thanks to Banneker, the city of Washington was built as it was designed.

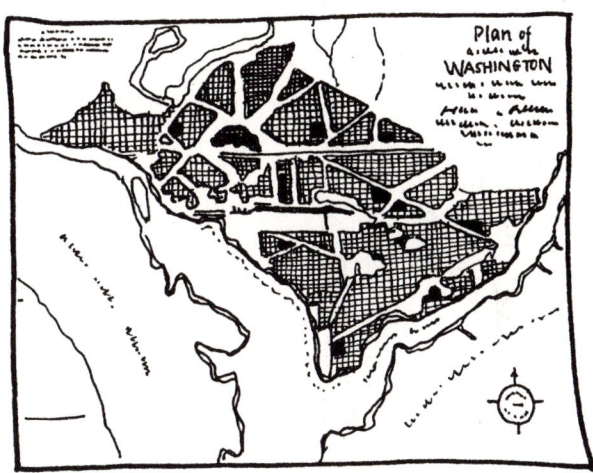

Find a cause and a chain of five effects in the passage. Write them on the map.

Cause   **Effects**

☐ → ☐ → ☐ → ☐ → ☐ → ☐

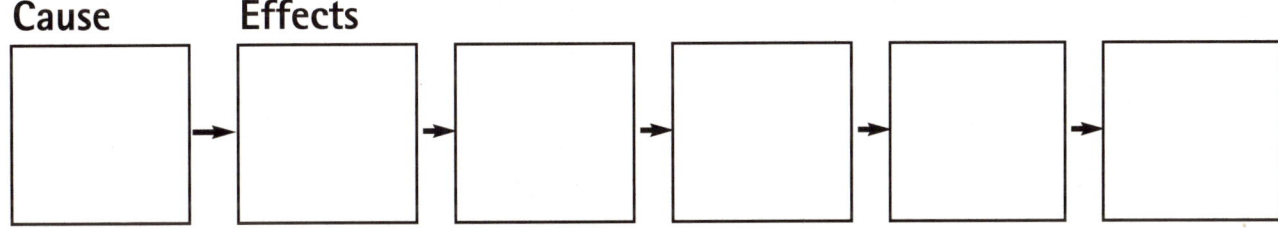

MORE! Make a list of the places you'd like to visit in Washington, D.C.

45

Name _____ Date _____

It's Corny

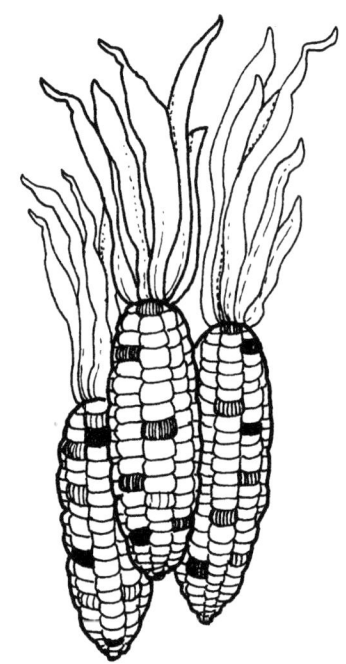

Want to see something corny? Then you should visit the Corn Palace, a public building in Mitchell, South Dakota. Every August, 13 new murals are placed on the walls of the Corn Palace. The murals are made from ears of corn! To create material for the murals, a local farmer has spent years developing different colors of corn. As a result, he now grows corn in at least nine colors, including red, blue, and brown. The farmer also spends a lot of time trying to outsmart the birds that peck at the murals! The people of Mitchell take great pride in the Corn Palace. After the murals are in place, thousands of tourists flock to Mitchell to see them. The tourists help boost the town's economy.

Find a cause and two chains of effects in the passage. Write them on the map.

Cause

Effects

MORE! Write a letter of advice to the farmer in Mitchell. Suggest how he might keep the birds away from the corn murals.

Name _____ Date _____

Testing It Out

Use after completing It's Corny on page 46.
Fill in the circle of the best answer.

1. Tourists visit Mitchell to—
   - Ⓐ boost the town's economy
   - Ⓑ put up new corn pictures
   - Ⓒ buy different-colored corn
   - Ⓓ see the Corn Palace murals

2. The Corn Palace murals have caused a local farmer to—
   - Ⓐ grow different colors of corn
   - Ⓑ harvest his corn early
   - Ⓒ eat a lot of corn
   - Ⓓ become a tourist

3. From the passage, you can guess that birds—
   - Ⓐ like to see murals
   - Ⓑ like to eat corn
   - Ⓒ want to visit with tourists
   - Ⓓ want to help the economy

4. One result of the Corn Palace murals is—
   - Ⓐ lack of corn
   - Ⓑ pride in the town
   - Ⓒ empty streets
   - Ⓓ plain corn

5. It is likely that the Corn Palace was built to promote—
   - Ⓐ summer
   - Ⓑ art
   - Ⓒ corn
   - Ⓓ birds

6. By May or June, the murals are probably—
   - Ⓐ looking colorful
   - Ⓑ smelling fresh
   - Ⓒ painted over
   - Ⓓ pecked clean

7. New murals probably go up in August because that's when the—
   - Ⓐ mural designs are ready
   - Ⓑ corn is harvested
   - Ⓒ birds are hungry
   - Ⓓ farmers have free time

8. The passage suggests that tourists in Mitchell—
   - Ⓐ enjoy birds
   - Ⓑ grow corn
   - Ⓒ like summer
   - Ⓓ spend money

Answers
Accept all reasonable answers.

p. 6 Details: recall 100 names and faces; memorize strings of numbers; recall order of a deck of cards

p. 7 Details: Whorl: like circles within circles; Tented Arch: like very steep hills; Loop: lines curve around and form patterns like loops

p. 8 Details: ice skating; sleigh riding; ninepins (or bowling); dying Easter eggs

p. 9 Details: dangerous to ships because not visible; found near North and South Poles; moved by currents and wind; nicknamed "growlers"; could provide water to deserts

p. 10 Topic: July 4th; Details: U.S. independence day; President Calvin Coolidge's birthday; "America" first sung in public; Washington Monument begun; death of Thomas Jefferson

p. 11 Topic: Materials in a Pencil; Details: graphite and clay; cedar; minerals; aluminum; soybean oil; latex

p. 12 Topic: Towns With "Bird Names"; Details: Egg Harbor, Wisconsin; Goose Creek, Oregon; Buzzards Bay, Massachusetts; Cuckoo, Virginia; Red Wing, Minnesota; Bird City, Kansas

p. 13 Topic: Uses of Radar; Details: air traffic control; burglar alarms; predict weather; measure baseball pitch speed; detect speeders; microwave ovens

p. 14 Topic: Visual Guidelines for Food Servings; Details: medium potato = computer mouse; cup of fruit = baseball; cup of chopped vegetables = fist; average bagel = hockey puck; 3 ounces meat = bar of soap; 3 ounces fish = checkbook

p. 15 1. B 2. A 3. D 4. B 5. A 6. D 7. A 8. C

p. 16 Tapping Sticks: drums, xylophones; Blowing Air: bagpipes, trumpets, trombones; Strings: guitars, lutes, sitars, violins

p. 17 Igneus: basalt, pumice, granite; Sedimentary: limestone, sandstone, chalk; Metamorphic: marble, slate

p. 18 Roofs: hipped, gabled, mansard; Windows: casement, sash, French, skylight; Doors: screen, sliding, storm

p. 19 ABBREVIATIONS; People: Mr. = mister, CEO = chief executive officer, Dr. = doctor; Places: Pk. = park, Rd. = road, Mt. = mountain, Dr. = drive; Measurement: tsp. = teaspoon, gal. = gallon

p. 20 BURNING CALORIES; Up to 89 calories: running, gymnastics; 43-88 calories: sweeping, walking, climbing stairs; 20-40 calories: writing, watching TV, eating, reading

p. 21 PREFIXES; dis- (not): disloyal, dishonest, disagree; re- (again): redo, rebuild, reconsider, renew; over- (too much): overjoyed, oversleep, overflow, overworked

p. 22 FOOD IN ANCIENT EGYPT; Breads: garlic, raisin, nut; Fruit: figs, dates, pomegranates; Vegetables: lettuce, beans, onions, cucumbers, leeks

p. 23 1. C 2. D 3. C 4. A 5. B 6. A 7. B 8. D

p. 24 1936-Caddie Woodlawn, 1961-Island of the Blue Dolphins, 1979-The Westing Game, 1984-Dear Mr. Henshaw, 2000-Bud, Not Buddy

p. 25 1927-colored bathtubs and sinks, 1935-color photographs, 1953-color TV, 1968-The Yellow Submarine, 1970- "Bein' Green"

p. 26 1785-George Washington's tulip poplars, 1823-Lewis and Clark's black locusts, 1843-Thoreau's red maples, 1863- Gettysburg honey locust, 1912-Washington D.C. cherry trees

p. 27 1901-initials on cars, 1903-first license plates, 1905-first auto theft, 1911-first 500-mile race, 1912-electric headlights, 1918-first white sidewall tires, 1935-parking meters

p. 28 1845-first baseball club, 1860-croquet, 1861-first college football game, 1863-roller skates, 1874-lawn tennis, 1878-bicycles, 1891-basketball, 1893-ice hockey

p. 29 1811-first ferry service, 1846-first organized baseball game, 1870-first boardwalk, 1877-first phonograph, 1878-first submarine, 1879-first incandescent lamp, 1884-first yacht club, 1889-first motion picture

p. 30 1789-Washington, first president; 1800-John Adams, first in White House, 1833-Jackson, first on train; 1849-Polk, first photographed; 1891-Harrison, first to have electricity; 1925-Coolidge, first radio broadcast; 1955-Eisenhower, first on color TV; 1993-Clinton, first e-mail

p. 31 1. B 2. D 3. A 4. C 5. D 6. B 7. C 8. D

p. 32 North Dakota: International Peace Garden; borders Canada/Both: on Great Plains; Dakota in names/South Dakota: Mt. Rushmore and Black Hills; Badlands National Park; Custer State Park

p. 33 Temperate: mild climates; along coasts/Both: cool, dry conditions/Boreal: spruce; hemlock; fir; northern regions

p. 34 1900: masks with solid steel grill; no leg guards; bulky gloves; heavy chest pads/Both: stand behind home plate; wear deer skin masks; wear chest pads; use gloves/2000: ultra-light masks; helmets; shin guards; molded gloves; form-fitting foam chest guard

p. 35 Fahrenheit: named after German physicist Gabriel Daniel Fahrenheit; invented early 1700s; freezing point 32°F; boiling point 212°F; used mostly in U.S./Both: named after scientists; invented in 1700s; measure temperature/Celsius: named after Swedish astronomer Anders Celsius; invented 1742; freezing point 0°C; boiling point 100°C; called centigrade scale; used in most countries

p. 36 Earth: oxygen; 24-hour day; has moon/Both: planets; made of rock; no rings/Venus: carbon dioxide; 116-day day; nearer to sun; no moon

p. 37 Warm front: warm air moves toward cold; lighter than cold air; slides over cold air; may cause rain or other precipitation/Both: boundary of mass of moving air/Cold front: cold air moves toward warm; heavier than warm air; slides under warm air; may cause thunderstorms

p. 38 Ch'usok: Korean holiday; more than 1,000 years old; remember ancestors; eat rice cakes, fruit, vegetable soup/Both: fall harvest holidays; time for giving thanks; family gathering/Thanksgiving: American holiday; since 1621; eat turkey, cranberries, potatoes, stuffing, vegetables, pumpkin pie; give thanks for freedoms

p. 39 1. C 2. D 3. C 4. B 5. B 6. D 7. A 8. B

p. 40 Effects: Public Roads Administration reroutes highways; tourist maps show elf haunts

p. 41 Effects: no mail delivery; directions refer to landmarks; pizza delivery can be slow

p. 42 Causes: good exercise; see city sights; assert pedestrian rights; meet community members; enjoy the night; Effect: people walk together at night as Moonwalkers

p. 43 Cause: McCoy invents oil cup for train cars. Effects: trains didn't have to stop for oiling; machine no good unless it has a McCoy oil cup; engineers demand "the real McCoy"; phrase means "the real thing"

p. 44 Cause: Birdseye goes ice-fishing on very cold day. Effects: Fish freezes when he pulls it from lake; fish begins to swim after thawing; Birdseye experiments with freezing and preserving other foods; he starts a frozen food company.

p. 45 Cause: L'Enfant wouldn't show plans for Washington D.C. to anyone but assistants. Effects: He's fired; he returns to France with plans; Americans are upset; Banneker redraws plans; city is completed.

p. 46 Cause: New murals placed in Corn Palace every August. Effects: Farmer develops colored corn; he grows nine colors of corn; he tries to keep birds from pecking murals. Effects: Townspeople are proud; tourists visit; tourists help economy.

p. 47 1. D 2. A 3. B 4. B 5. C 6. D 7. B 8. D

48